OC 13 '06	DATE DUE	
AP 28 '06		
OC 21 '06		
NOV 1 6 '10		

20TH CENTURY MEDIA

40s & 50s

POWER AND PERSUASION

Please visit our web site at: www.garethstevens.com
For a free color catalog describing Gareth Stevens Publishing's
list of high-quality books and multimedia programs, call
1-800-542-2595 (USA) or 1-800-387-3178 (Canada).
Gareth Stevens Publishing's fax: (414) 332-3567.

Library of Congress Cataloging-in-Publication Data

Parker, Steve.
    20th century media / by Steve Parker.
        v. cm.
    Includes bibliographical references and index.
    Contents: [1] 1900–20: print to pictures. [2] 20s & 30s: entertainment for all.
  [3] 40s & 50s: power and persuasion. [4] 1960s: the Satellite Age. [5] 70s & 80s:
  global technology. [6] 1990s: electronic media.
    ISBN 0-8368-3182-9 (v. 1: lib. bdg.) — ISBN 0-8368-3183-7 (v. 2: lib. bdg.) —
  ISBN 0-8368-3184-5 (v. 3: lib. bdg.) — ISBN 0-8368-3185-3 (v. 4: lib. bdg.) —
  ISBN 0-8368-3186-1 (v. 5: lib. bdg.) — ISBN 0-8368-3187-X (v. 6: lib. bdg.)
    1. Mass media—History—20th century—Juvenile literature. [1. Mass
  media—History—20th century.] I. Title: Twentieth century media. II. Title.
  P91.2.P37   2002
  302.23'09'04—dc21   2002022556

This North American edition first published in 2002 by
Gareth Stevens Publishing
A World Almanac Education Group Company
330 West Olive Street, Suite 100
Milwaukee, Wisconsin 53212 USA

Original edition © 2002 by David West Children's Books. First published in Great Britain
in 2002 by Heinemann Library, Halley Court, Jordan Hill, Oxford OX2 8EJ, a division of Reed
Educational and Professional Publishing Limited. This U.S. edition © 2002 by Gareth Stevens, Inc.
Additional end matter © 2002 by Gareth Stevens, Inc.

Designer: Rob Shone
Editor: James Pickering
Picture Research: Carrie Haines

Gareth Stevens Editor: Dorothy L. Gibbs

Photo Credits:
Abbreviations: (t) top, (m) middle, (b) bottom, (l) left, (r) right

The Advertising Archive Ltd.: pages 22(tl), 23(t, m).
The Art Archive/Imperial War Museum WM: page 9(bl); D. C. Thomson cpt.: page 17(m, r, b);
  Eileen Tweedy: cover (br), page 28(l).
Corbis Stock Market: pages 4(b), 5(r), 6(b), 7(tr), 8(b), 10-11, 14(m), 18(b), 20(tl), 23(br), 29(tr).
The Culture Archive: pages 11(tr), 24(r), 27(b).
Mary Evans Picture Library: pages 4(tr), 16(m).
Hulton Archive: pages 6(l), 8(t), 10(m), 12(both), 12-13, 13(tr), 14(tl), 26(tr).
The Kobal Collection: pages 7(bl), 18(tl), 18-19, 19(b).
Popperfoto: cover (m), pages 3, 5(bl), 7(br), 9(t-all, br), 10(bl), 13(b-both), 15(all), 20(br), 20-21, 22(b),
  26(b), 27(t), 28(tr), 29(ml, br).
Redferns/Michael Ochs Archives: page 21(br).
Rex Features/Leonard McCombe/Time Pix: page 25(mr).
Frank Spooner Pictures: page 25(br).
Topham Picturepoint: pages 11(bl), 16(bl, tr), 17(tl), 19(tr), 24(l); Associated Press: page 21(t).
Vin Mag Archive Ltd.: page 25(t).
Vogue/Condé Nast Publications Ltd.: page 27(m).

Printed in the United States of America

1 2 3 4 5 6 7 8 9 06 05 04 03 02

20ᵀᴴ CENTURY MEDIA

40s & 50s

POWER AND PERSUASION

Steve Parker

Gareth Stevens Publishing
A WORLD ALMANAC EDUCATION GROUP COMPANY

CONTENTS

THRILL-PACKED STORIES OF THE FUTURE!

AMAZING STORIES

PRICE IN GT. BRITAIN 1'6

When Two Worlds Meet

Print publications changed dramatically in the 1950s with the rapid growth of special-interest magazines and periodicals on subjects ranging from sports to science fiction.

Throughout the 1950s, television technology advanced at great speed. TV cameras moved out of the studio to cover outdoor activities, such as sports events.

WAR AND PEACE

In 1940, World War II was spreading to involve huge areas of the world in its death and destruction. Twenty years later, much had changed. The horrors and hardships of international conflict had faded, and many regions were entering a new era of peace and prosperity.

Significant changes were happening in the media, too, especially in television. Before 1940, television hardly existed. By 1960, millions of homes in wealthier countries, such as the United States and Britain, had TV sets — and daily life changed forever. To compete with TVs, radios became smaller, lighter, and portable. To compete with broadcast media, print media introduced a new generation of specialized periodicals. And all of the mass media discovered a new, fast-growing market — teenagers!

Improvments in special effects were, at least partly, the reason for a 1950s boom in science-fiction movies.

5

During World War II, many countries used radio to raise the spirits of the public with comedy and cheerful songs. This scene from a radio studio in 1941 shows the famous British comedy It's That Man Again (ITMA) *in progress.*

KING OF THE WORLD

Today, global superstars come and go almost weekly, but in the 1950s, they were few and far between. Even fewer were young. In the United States, in January 1956, the voice of a young Tennessee truck driver, just turning twenty-one, shook the world with his first musical hit, "Heartbreak Hotel."

MEDIA SATURATION

By the end of that same year, Mississippi-born Elvis Presley (1935–1977) had chalked up eight No. 1 hits on the U. S. record charts. Not only was his voice instantly recognized in almost every Western nation, but also his pictures were everywhere — on posters, record jackets, magazines, and books. He also appeared on television and in movies. These days, this kind of publicity would be called "saturation" media coverage.

RENÉ CHATEAU presents

ELVIS PRESLEY

KING CREOLE

In Presley's first movies, between 1956 and 1958, he usually played himself. He was a rough and ready, rising rock 'n' roll star, admired by boys and adored by girls.

GUIDING STAR

Elvis was guided by a cunning manager, Colonel Tom Parker, who used every media opportunity to keep Presley in the public eye. Parker also controlled much of Elvis's private life. By the mid-1970s, however, Elvis had drifted into substance abuse, put on weight, and was performing mostly cabaret shows.

Parker and Presley

THE COMEBACK "KING"

Elvis quickly became "the king" of rock 'n' roll. Even being drafted into the U. S. Army in 1958 just gave him more media coverage. For most of the 1960s, however, his records and movies were less memorable. Then, in a 1968 Christmas television show, he returned to his original, aggressive, hip-swiveling, lip-curling style. In a 1973 live TV performance from Honolulu, Elvis was watched by over a billion people.

THE YOUTH CULTURE

Elvis triumphed in music, in movies, and on television — and he was young! After the hardships of World War II, young people of the 1950s had more time and money than the youth of past generations had. The youth of the 1950s also had TVs to watch and records to buy. Such advantages helped Elvis become the first multimedia megastar and gave young people a culture of their own.

The young Presley's relaxed style and easygoing humor made his interviews very entertaining.

Getting his long hair cut short for the army was yet another photo opportunity for Elvis Presley.

In 1956, Elvis's first film, Love Me Tender, *introduced his smoldering good looks to the moviegoing public.*

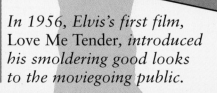

FRONTLINE NEWS

Modern media can cover news live, as it happens, on radio, television, and, increasingly, the Internet. During World War II, only radio could offer instant reports. Most people kept up with current events by reading newspapers and magazines and by watching short films called newsreels, which were usually shown before the main movie feature at a cinema.

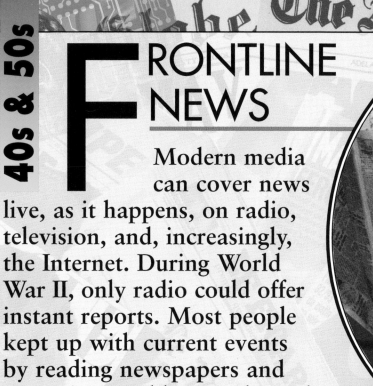

FINAL MORNING EXTRA
San Francisco Chronicle

U.S. AT WAR!
Japs Bomb Hawaii, Philippines, Invade Thailand, Malaya; U.S. Battleships Claimed Sunk; FDR Talks to Congress Today!

In December 1941, Americans read about the Japanese attack on U. S. warships at Pearl Harbor in Hawaii. The attack brought the United States into World War II.

American war correspondent Ernie Pyle (1900–1945) wrote about the personal lives of U. S. soldiers and the terrors they suffered. Pyle was killed with forces fighting in the Pacific in 1945.

RESPONSIBLE REPORTING

When a country is at war, the media encounter new pressures. Reporting all events completely and truthfully might not be wise. If enemies found out about secret plans, thousands of lives would be put at risk. In World War II, news media, especially radio and newspapers, followed government guidelines about what should and should not be revealed. Posters, announcements, slogans, and songs encouraged citizens to support the troops fighting abroad and to smile in spite of the hardships at home.

LEGENDS IN THE MAKING

Many news correspondents became famous media figures after the war. U. S. radio reporter Edward Murrow (1908–1965) moved to television during the anticommunist McCarthy era in the late 1940s and early 1950s. American journalist Walter Cronkite (*b.* 1916) became a legendary anchorman with CBS television. In Britain, newspaper reporter Richard Dimbleby (1913–1965) became the "Voice of the BBC." All of these media "legends" were known for their sincere approach to discovering the truth.

"Keep it under your hat!"

CARELESS TALK COSTS LIVES

Posters put up in public places displayed slogans urging people to help the war effort and to be aware of spies.

9

WAR NEWS — AND VIEWS

Perhaps the most widely read news correspondent of the time was Ernie Pyle. Pyle wrote about the lives and deaths of ordinary U. S. soldiers, bringing the terrible human tragedy of war home to millions of people.

Almost any item could be used to help win the war. These Japanese matchboxes were meant to arouse feelings against Britain and the United States.

PROPAGANDA

To support a cause, information may be very selective, distorted, or even outright lies. This kind of information is called propaganda. Each country in World War II had its share. As part of Germany's anti-British propaganda, U. S.-born William Joyce (1906–1946) broadcasted on the radio, in English, as Lord Haw-Haw. Joyce was hanged for treason.

Lord Haw-Haw laughed at British listeners — "haw haw."

CHANNELS GALORE

During the 1950s, the furniture in millions of living rooms was being rearranged. People no longer sat gazing at the flames of a fire or around the piano or the radio. They had a new focal point — the television.

In 1955, NBC's "Peter Pan," starring actress-singer Mary Martin (right), was the first TV show to attract over 60 million viewers.

Early TV sets were big and bulky. Many had doors on the front or foldaway tops to look like furniture pieces such as cabinets or desks.

TV'S REACH

The new medium of television first became popular in the United States, which was a wealthy country with a rich tradition of entertainment. The first coast-to-coast broadcasts in the United States came in 1951. U. S. trends in technology and types of programming quickly spread across the Atlantic, especially to Britain and other European countries. Intense competition to have the greatest number of viewers led television networks to go after more advertising income.

10

CHEATERS!

In the war to attract viewers, the prize money awarded on 1950s quiz shows reached enormous amounts. Then, Herbert Stempel, who had been a champion on the leading quiz show *Twenty-One*, revealed that some contestants were given the answers and told how to act. A huge public outcry led to new laws to guard against cheating on radio and television.

Stempel's successor, Charles van Doren, pretends to know the answer to a question on Twenty-One.

From 1955 to 1959, Phil Silvers starred in Sergeant Bilko, *a popular Sunday-night comedy series.*

The most popular TV show of the 1950s was I Love Lucy, *starring Lucille Ball and her husband, Desi Arnaz. Shown in over 100 countries, some episodes of this family comedy series attracted nine out of every ten television viewers.*

SOAPS AND GAMES

An early success for television was the soap opera. Its ongoing stories and commercials for soap powders and other household cleaning products were designed to appeal to those watching TV at home, during the day. In about 1954, big-money quiz shows, such as *The $64,000 Question* and *Twenty-One*, started to draw large audiences, too.

CHANGING HABITS

Most early television was broadcasted live or recorded on movie-style film. With the arrival of videotape in 1956, programs could be recorded and edited for later broadcasting. As people sat down to watch their favorite shows and, from 1954, eat their TV dinners, daily habits began to change.

COLOR TV

By the late 1940s, testing had started on color television, to replace black-and-white. Inside a color TV tube, tiny atomic particles called electrons were fired from "guns" in three streams, or beams. A magnetic coil made the beams scan across a screen through small holes in a mask. Tiny dots of phosphor, in three colors, glowed when hit by the electrons.

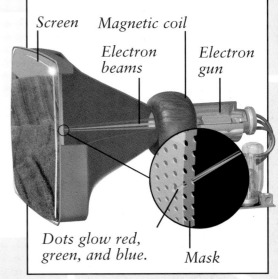

Screen   *Magnetic coil*

Electron beams   *Electron gun*

Dots glow red, green, and blue.   *Mask*

NETWORK POWER

As television grew, so did its power, with network bosses deciding each program's content and approach. A program that criticized a politician, for example, could badly damage, or even ruin, that person's reputation and career.

EXPOSED ON-SCREEN

In 1954, U. S. Senator Joseph McCarthy went on TV to defend his anticommunist witch-hunts — but his plan backfired. On-screen, for all to see, McCarthy showed himself as a scheming bully who used the media for highly personal, and often unjustified, attacks.

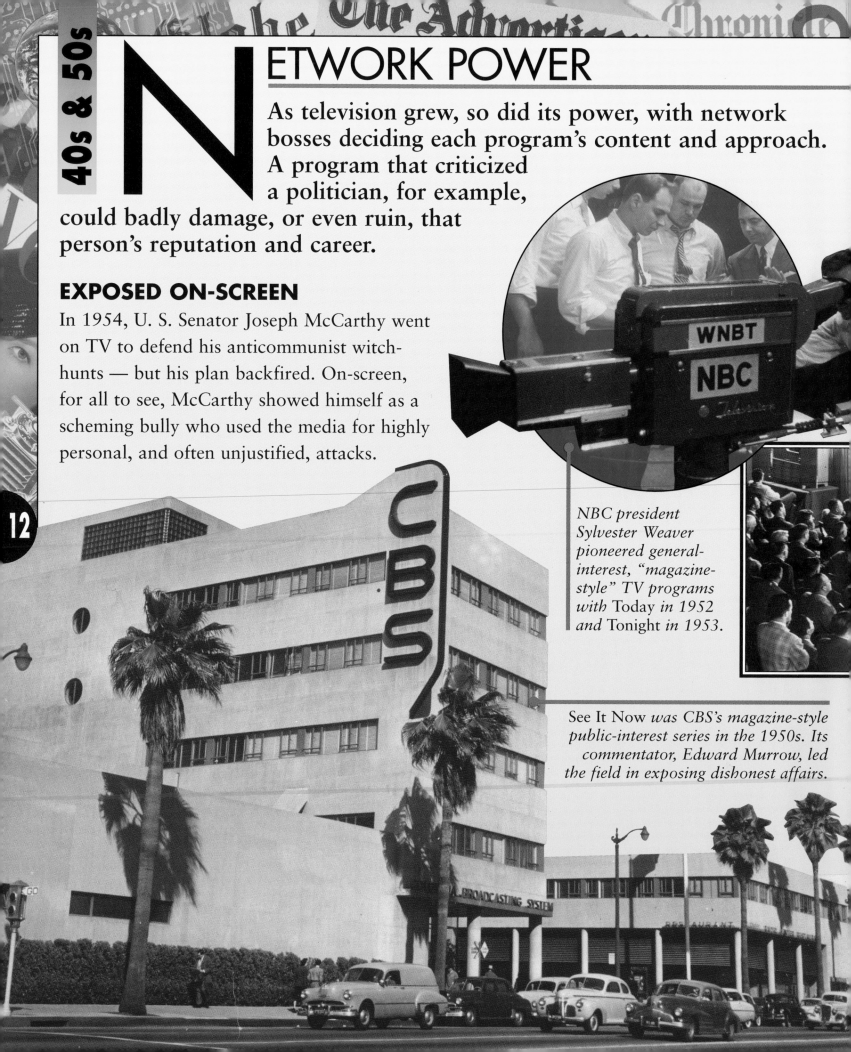

NBC president Sylvester Weaver pioneered general-interest, "magazine-style" TV programs with Today *in 1952 and* Tonight *in 1953.*

See It Now *was CBS's magazine-style public-interest series in the 1950s. Its commentator, Edward Murrow, led the field in exposing dishonest affairs.*

SWEET SUCCESS

Power struggles between TV networks were particularly fierce in the United States. The two biggest rivals were the Columbia Broadcasting System (CBS) and the National Broadcasting Company (NBC), which was owned by radio and recording giant RCA. In 1943, the American Broadcasting Company (ABC) also became a contender. ABC was funded by Edward Noble, who had made a fortune manufacturing candy.

In 1946, there were about 6,000 TV sets in the United States. Five years later, there were 12 million. Even some movie theaters had installed "public" sets.

DIFFERENT SYSTEMS

The U. S. television networks competed for viewers and advertisers — and not always honestly. The British Broadcasting Corporation (BBC) was more independent. Because it was funded by license fees, there was no need to attract advertising money.

TV was an important medium for advertisers. The 1958 U. S. Senate election was sponsored by a baking company.

LOOKING GOOD, SOUNDING GOOD

The first live debates between major politicians were televised in 1960. Richard M. Nixon and John F. Kennedy debated to win the most votes in that year's presidential election. Many TV viewers preferred Kennedy, while most radio listeners were persuaded by Nixon, showing the impact a visual image can have.

Nixon (left) and Kennedy held four live, televised debates in 1960.

RADIO GOES MOBILE

The growth of television greatly affected radio during the 1950s. Between 1949 and 1952, *Amos 'n' Andy*, one of the top-rated radio comedies in the United States, lost more than half of its listeners. Radio bosses fought back.

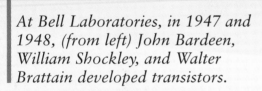

At Bell Laboratories, in 1947 and 1948, (from left) John Bardeen, William Shockley, and Walter Brattain developed transistors.

SMALLER AND SMALLER

Radio got an unexpected boost from the transistor, a new electronic device. A transistor's job was similar to a valve's, but a transistor was smaller and lighter, and it needed less electricity. Transistors could be used in all kinds of electrical equipment, but they were especially useful in radios. With transistors instead of valves, engineers could build smaller, portable, battery-powered receivers. The first mass-produced transistor radio, from Sony, went on sale in 1952.

Using a portable disk cutter or a tape recorder, a radio reporter could record a story almost anywhere and broadcast it at a later time.

ON THE MOVE

Although TVs also began to use transistors, the sets were still big and heavy, and they needed electricity and a large aerial, or antenna, to receive broadcasts. So, television sets had to stay at home. Radios, however, became small enough to carry almost anywhere. They provided news and entertainment on the move, especially in cars, which were also increasing in number.

VALVES vs. TRANSISTORS

Doing much the same tasks as the triode valve, the transistor's main job was to strengthen, or amplify, a varying pattern of electricity. While valves, however, were big, heavy, hot, and used lots of electricity, transistors were small, lightweight, and cool. Transistors were tougher and more reliable than delicate valves, too.

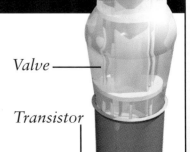

Valve

Transistor

A small, portable radio made with transistors soon became known as a "tranny." This suitcase design copies the carryalls or vanity cases of the time.

By 1954, radios were small enough to carry on bicycles. This version had a handlebar loudspeaker and crossbar batteries. Safety, however, was a problem.

MADCAP FUN

A radio show needed no costumes, makeup, or scenery so, compared to television, it cost very little. Low costs meant radio could afford to experiment with new ideas. The BBC's *The Goon Show* (1951–1959) began a tradition of zany humor and silly voices, borrowed partly from movie comedies such as those of the Marx Brothers. The Goons, in turn, inspired TV shows of the 1960s, such as *Monty Python's Flying Circus*.

The "Goons" (clockwise from top, center) were Spike Milligan, Peter Sellers, Harry Secombe, and Michael Bentine.

ON THE SPOT

Radio had another way to compete with TV — its news reporters could rush quickly to almost any location. Transporting and setting up large cameras and other machinery for television took a long time, so radio gained a reputation for being first with the news. Radio also had more stations than TV had channels, and radio offered a wider choice of programming.

PAPERS AND MAGS

PIn the 1920s, newspapers and magazines survived the radio boom partly by using that new medium. They printed listings of radio programs and time schedules and feature articles about radio shows and major stars. In the 1950s, they did the same for TV.

Amazing Stories, *the world's first science-fiction magazine, was founded in 1926, so by 1950, it had a wealth of experience in imaginative ideas, gripping storylines, and interesting illustration styles. It took several years for TV and movies to catch up.*

16

THRILL-PACKED STORIES OF THE FUTURE!

AMAZING STORIES

PRICE IN 1'6 GT. BRITAIN

...wo Worlds Meet

...T MOORE WILLIAMS

RADIO TIMES

JOURNAL OF THE BBC

BBC Morning, Afternoon, and Evening Programmes: MAY 4-10

PRICE TWOPENCE

BRITAIN'S CRISIS

THE CHALLENGE TO ACTION : : WAYS AND MEANS

This "listings" magazine started in about 1923. It contained the times of all BBC radio programs. In the 1940s, it began to include television programs but kept its Radio Times *name.*

MORE MAGS

To compete with radio and television, magazines and periodicals developed in two main ways. One of the ways was producing publications that "fed" off of broadcast media. A flurry of new magazines and journals listed radio and television program schedules, reviewed shows, and went behind the scenes to gather gossip and expose problems. Radio and TV fought back by producing programs that "fed" off of the print media.

SEE

15¢ JULY 1952

HOW TO ELECT A REPUBLICAN PRESIDENT
by Harold E. Stassen

MARILYN MONROE

TERROR IN THE MIDDLE EAST
by John Roy Carlson

INGRID BERGMAN TODAY

THE TRUTH ABOUT AIR CRASHES
by Senator Owen Brewster

Magazines such as Time, Life, Fortune, *and* See *contained articles about radio, TV, and movies. This 1952 issue of* See *featured Marilyn Monroe, who, at that time, was an up-and-coming movie actress.*

NEWS AND PRESS AGENCIES

It would be far too costly for every newspaper, radio station, and TV channel to send its own reporter to every news event, so news and press agencies attend major events and sell the information to the various media. Each medium alters the details to fit its own approach. In 1958, two big agencies, the United Press Association and the International News Service, joined to form United Press International, an agency to rival the Associated Press (*f.* 1848) and London's Reuters (*f.* 1851).

Reuters' newsroom in London (1951)

SPECIALIZED MAGS

A second development by magazines and periodicals was more specialized titles. Today, we have magazines on almost every imaginable subject, but people in the 1950s did not. Publishers were just beginning to explore single-interest subjects, dealing with only one topic in great detail. In the United States, *Sports Illustrated*, which started in 1954, was a pioneer.

MORE SPECIALIZED MAGS

In a time of hazy television pictures, without slow motion or instant replay, *Sports Illustrated* attracted readers with its high-quality photos and careful analyses of sports topics and events. Many similar magazines quickly followed, some specializing in just a single sport. The trend spread to other interests, too, including cars, cooking, gardening, and movies. Special children's publications also flourished, as popular radio and TV characters found their way into print.

A successful character, such as an amusing cat, could begin in almost any medium — comic books, magazines, radio, television. Other media could then buy a license to adapt the character.

AT THE MOVIES

Before World War II, Hollywood filmmakers dominated the movie scene. Although still powerful after the war, they suffered from television's popularity, problems linked to politics, and an increasing interest in films from other countries.

Musicals such as Guys and Dolls (1955), starring Marlon Brando and Frank Sinatra, helped moviegoers "escape" for a time.

PROBLEMS, PROBLEMS

Movies had been helped by newsreels, the short films about current events that were shown as features before a main movie. Now, however, people could watch the news at home, on television. As if that problem was not enough, the anticommunist antics of U. S. Senator Joseph McCarthy had spread politics to entertainment. Some of Hollywood's leading actors and directors, such as Orson Welles and Charlie Chaplin, were denounced as "un-American." As arguments raged, Hollywood lost its grip on the movie business.

The Fly (1958) was part of a trend toward science-fiction movies and stories of terror that featured weird costumes and special effects.

ANIMATED FILMS

U. S. animator Walt Disney's first major character was Mickey Mouse, originally named Mortimer Mouse, in 1928. Disney himself provided Mickey's squeaky voice. By 1940, the Disney corporation had produced a string of remarkable animated movies. In 1940, *Fantasia* set Mickey's and other Disney characters' movements to classical music. *Pinocchio*, *Dumbo*, and *Bambi* followed within two years. Later, Disney started producing adventure films with human actors, such as *Treasure Island* (1950).

Bambi's friends included a rabbit named Thumper.

MUSICAL FUN

The big U. S. movie studios continued, however, to produce successful films, especially glitzy musicals adapted from stage shows, such as *On the Town* (1949), *Oklahoma* and *Guys and Dolls* (1955), *The King and I* (1956), and *South Pacific* (1958). Movie musicals had an added benefit. The songs could be sold on vinyl disks, or records, another media format that was gaining popularity. Records and films helped each other make greater profits than either could alone.

WORLD CINEMA

New film styles came from European directors such as Ingmar Bergman, Francois Truffaut, and Frederico Fellini. Akira Kurosawa, in Japan, and Satyajit Ray, in India, also introduced fresh ideas to the mainly Western movie business.

In Ingmar Bergman's The Seventh Seal *(1956), Death comes to take a knight. To prove human goodness, the knight challenges Death to a beachside game of chess.*

Film director Akira Kurosawa adapted tales of Japanese life and tradition to make epic movies such as The Seven Samurai *(1954).*

POPULAR MUSIC

The growth of radio during the 1930s created a dip in the sales of recorded music. The record industry fought back by replacing the standard five-minute, grooved disks with two new formats, the long play (LP) 33 and the single 45.

LONG AND SHORT

The numbers 33 and 45 refer to revolutions per minute (rpm), or how many times the disk spins around in one minute.

The 33, or LP, was developed by CBS in 1948. At 12 inches (30 centimeters) across, it held 20 minutes of sound on each side. In 1949, RCA introduced the 45 single, which was 7 inches (18 cm) across but had only up to five minutes of playing time on each side. The new record formats improved sales for different reasons.

With both record players and 45-rpm singles available at affordable prices, homes, especially in the United States, had more modern music in them.

Charts listing each week's best-selling records appeared in the 1950s. In Britain, the New Musical Express's first "Hit Parade" came out on November 14, 1952, and the song "Here in My Heart," by Al Martino, was at the top of it.

CLASSIC AND "POP"

The 33-rpm LP was used mainly for longer pieces of classical music and songs from stage and movie musicals. The 45-rpm disk was called a "single" because it usually had only one song on each side. Singles cost far less than LPs, so they were within the price range of many young people. Increasing record sales and competition within the new generation of recording stars led to popular, or "pop," music and weekly "charts."

ROCK 'N' ROLL

Many established singers of the 1940s, such as Frank Sinatra and Bing Crosby, sang relaxed ballads or swing tunes with big-band orchestras. As usual, younger people wanted something different. That "something" came in the form of rock 'n' roll, which was a blend of many other musical styles, including bouncy rhythm and blues (R&B), doo-wop, rockabilly, and jazz. Rock 'n' roll exploded into the 1950s youth culture. It was fast, noisy, exciting — and it annoyed older people.

Alan Freed (1922–1965)

RADIO DJs

Young people in the 1950s listened to transistor radios in cars, in their bedrooms, and even on the beach. They also bought records, so the two media, both radio and records, benefited. Personalities called disk jockeys (DJs) presented radio music shows. In the United States, Alan Freed, a DJ both in Cleveland, Ohio, (1950–1954) and in New York, introduced music with black origins to a wide audience and invented the term "rock 'n' roll." Freed's career ended, however, in 1959, when he was accused of taking money for playing certain records.

Bill Haley and the Comets, who were formerly country-style musicians, made rock 'n' roll popular with hits such as "Rock Around the Clock" (1954).

Rock 'n' roll was not the only popular music in the 1950s. Established singers, such as Peggy Lee, sold millions of records to older listeners. The song "Fever" was one of Lee's biggest hits.

Calling All GIRLS

Largest Circulation
Magazine For Girls
.. more than ½ million

MAY 1945

COMICS · FASHIONS · THINGS TO DO · GOOD LOOKS · MOVIES · **STORIES**

Magazines for teenagers were a fast-growing area of print media. They contained tips on makeup, fashion, hairstyles, and romance.

A NEW MEDIA MARKET

The word "teenager" first came into use during the 1950s. It described young people with more time, more money, and more freedom than ever before. Teenagers were a gold mine for the media, and by 1960, there were millions of them.

GROUP IDENTITY

People who were no longer children, but were not quite adults, had long been without any identity as a group. They were usually caught up in daily hardships ranging from work to war. In the 1950s, however, especially in Western countries, living was easier, parents were wealthier, and "teenagers," with easy access to radio, television, movies, magazines, and music, developed their own interests and created an entirely new culture.

Movies and other media reflected teenage culture. The Blackboard Jungle (1955) featured rock 'n' roll and rebellious students.

NOW FOR THE FIRST TIME YOU CAN SEE

COLUMBIA PICTURES Presents

A STANLEY KRAMER PRODUCTION

MARLON BRANDO as

THE WILD ONE

with MARY MURPHY · ROBERT KEITH and LEE MARVIN

Screenplay by JOHN PAXTON
Directed by LASLO BENEDEK

Teenagers became a new subgroup of the population. With their own language and attitudes, they were different from both children and adults. In The Wild One (1954), *a movie about rebelling against authority, the star is asked, "What are you rebelling against?" "What've you got?" is the reply.*

New products and advertising were aimed at the teenage market. This print ad suggests that a soft drink will make a person successful with fast cars and the opposite sex.

IMPRESSIONABLE REBELS

Teenagers rebelled against tradition. They wanted to be different from their parents. They were at an impressionable age in a time when fashions and fads were changing rapidly, and they had cash, from allowances and part-time jobs. Media bosses quickly recognized that a brand new market was opening up for ever-changing products and programs.

SHARED INTERESTS

Gathering in groups at soda fountains and hamburger stands, teenagers read magazines, listened to rock 'n' roll on jukeboxes, and discussed their interests in movies, books, clothes, cars, and other important topics. They related to new, young music and movie stars, such as Elvis Presley, James Dean, and Marlon Brando, who dealt with teenage problems such as school, jobs, relationships, and rejecting authority. The media-based youth culture established in the 1950s still flourishes today.

"Soup up" the conversation with this quick, refreshing lift!

SWEET FREEDOM

For centuries, young women were expected to stay home, do chores, and go out only with the family. But with washing machines, vacuum cleaners, and other new, laborsaving gadgets, housework took much less time. So girls gained more independence and found many new ways to spend their money.

The soda fountain was a popular gathering place for teenage girls.

MEDIUM AND MESSAGE

Advertisements are so clever, sometimes, that we forget the products they are promoting. Remembering whether an ad was in a magazine or a newspaper, on television or radio, or at the movies is often easier.

Advertisements for home life products, such as food, beverages, appliances, and cleaning items, often showed what became known as the "nuclear family," which had two parents and two children, a boy and a girl, all unbelievably happy.

CHOOSING THE MEDIUM

In the 1950s, television was the newest, most high-tech medium to join the assortment of ways advertisers could reach the public — and wise advertisers flocked to it. The powerful, fast-moving, fashion-conscious advertising business involves the manufacturers who make the products, the advertising agencies that produce commercials for them, and the media that bring the ads to public attention. In the 1950s, just as today, advertising paid for much of a medium's content. Also, as now, the impression an ad made was greatly affected by the medium carrying it.

Advertising agencies were specialists in designing ads. In the process, an agency's media consultants decided which medium would best promote each of a client's products.

MAKING A MESSAGE

Television brought images, sounds, and actions right into people's homes, but producing TV ads cost huge amounts of money. Furthermore, after a TV commercial was shown, the viewer's attention quickly moved on to the next image. Ads in newspapers and magazines were longer lasting and could have coupons or order forms in them. As magazines became more specialized, advertisers could direct an ad to readers who were already interested in the product, rather than making a general appeal to the entire TV-viewing public.

POWER COMPANIES BUILD FOR YOUR FUTURE ELECTRIC LIVING

Advertisers in the 1950s hoped that people would soon be able to order products by speaking into microphones that were linked to their TVs and to telecommunication networks. Electronic shopping did not arrive until the 1990s, and it was done on computers, without microphones.

MEDIA GURU

Marshall McLuhan, a Canadian-born writer and teacher, published his first books in the 1950s. With powerful opinions on the use and effects of different media, McLuhan became one of the first media "gurus." His phrase "the medium is the message" meant that the form of communication could actually be more important than the information it carried.

Marshall McLuhan (1911–1980)

25

SEEING "SPOTS"

Advertisers quickly learned how to use costly television commercials. Networks sold time for "spot" ads, in which a region promoted its local products and services during a commercial break in a national show.

Many ads portrayed a perfect, dream-like world. The suggestion behind this ad's image is, if you buy the car, you will also gain big-city success and a rich lifestyle.

REAL-LIFE PHOTOS

During World War II, thousands of photographers, on all sides, recorded terrible scenes on the battlefields. Their pictures in newspapers and magazines showed the horror of war to people at home.

An early Polaroid Land Camera

LIFE IN BLACK AND WHITE

French-born Henri Cartier-Bresson (*b*. 1908) was one of the most influential photographers of the time. He rarely used indoor studio techniques or complex equipment. Instead, he traveled the world with small, portable cameras, often working outdoors, with black-and-white film rather than color. His method was to survey a scene, compose a picture in his mind, then wait for the precise moment to record it in real life.

In February 1945, U. S. troops invaded the Japanese-held Pacific island of Iwo Jima in one of World War II's bloodiest battles. An image of marines raising the U. S. flag on Iwo Jima has become a symbol of the war, often copied in movies and monuments. The original image was staged by photographer Joe Rosenthal after the actual battle had ended.

PHOTOJOURNALISM

Cartier-Bresson wanted to capture the details of ordinary daily life, writing, in documentary style, with pictures, as a photojournalist. In 1947, with Hungarian-American photographer Robert Capa and others, Cartier-Bresson founded Magnum Photos, an agency in which photographers from around the world worked together to control sales of their own pictures in the international marketplace.

INSTANT PICTURES

During the 1930s and 1940s, cameras became smaller, easier to use, and less expensive, but developing film to make prints was still done at a professional photo lab, and it took several days. In 1948, U. S. scientist Edwin Land (1909–1991) introduced the first "instant print" camera, the Polaroid Land Camera. The pictures developed automatically inside the camera and were ready to pull out in a minute or two.

Robert Capa (1913–1954), whose real name was André Friedman, took heart-stopping photographs of World War II. He saw life and death in Africa and Italy and waded ashore at Normandy, France, with the Allies on D-Day, June 6, 1944. Capa continued his war photojournalism into the 1950s. In 1954, he was killed by a land mine in Vietnam, during the Indochina War.

Fifties fashion magazines, such as Vogue *and* Harper's Bazaar, *had highly posed, carefully taken pictures on almost every page. The lack of background in the photos separated the images from the reality of daily life. Fashion magazines seemed to be aimed at the rich and famous but were bought by people who wanted to be rich and famous.*

FASHION PHOTOS

Far from war and its hardships, fashion photography developed into "high art," capturing the latest trends in clothing and makeup design. It could take days in the studio to produce a single picture, as tiny details of lighting or the folds of a garment were adjusted time and again. Richard Avedon and Irving Penn were leading U. S. fashion photographers. Avedon later took portraits of celebrities, too, but he used frontal views, pale backgrounds, and plain lighting to make them look more ordinary.

Among the specialty magazines that appeared in the 1950s were yearly, and even monthly, compilations of photographs. This photo is from a magazine of the best sports pictures of 1955.

THE COLD WAR

World War II ended in 1945 with great hopes for global peace and harmony. Yet, new conflicts flared, especially in eastern Asia, and two superpowers, the United States and the Soviet Union, entered a struggle called the "Cold War."

28

STALIN DEAD

STALIN DEAD!

Malenkov

STALIN DIES

Daily Worker

Dictator Succumbs

Herald Tribune

Stalin Is Dead

End Comes at Night 4 Days After Stroke

The New York Times.

STALIN DIES AFTER 29-YEAR RULE; HIS SUCCESSOR NOT ANNOUNCED; U. S. WATCHFUL, EISENHOWER SAYS

The world held its breath when longtime Soviet leader Joseph Stalin died, in 1953. Would the new leaders of the USSR be more friendly, or would the rift between East and West deepen?

STANDOFF

The capitalist, freedom-loving United States and its Western European allies faced the communist, state-controlled Soviet Union and its Eastern European and Asian allies, but these countries never waged a direct battle. Their "Cold War," a term invented in 1947 by U. S. journalist Herbert B. Swope, was fought mainly with words and images in the media. Each superpower tried to outdo the other in military might, economic strength, and the success of its political beliefs.

This poster produced by the United Nations shows the supposed dangers of communism in graphic form. A shadowy, rifle-toting, North Korean soldier looms over ordinary South Korean citizens who are being marched into communist "slavery."

MENACE AT THE MOVIES

Propaganda is highly selective or distorted information used to support a cause. Both the East and the West used it in many forms during the Cold War. In movies by Western filmmakers, villains, even from outer space, had the facial features, sound-alike names, and look-alike clothing of communists. Books described battles that were thinly disguised versions of the real East-West standoff. In the East, roles were reversed. Western-looking "bad guys" were portrayed as loudmouthed, loose-living, and stupid.

It Came from Outer Space *(1953)*

U. S. soldiers prepare print materials to drop from airplanes over Korea. The highly anticommunist message told about the dangers of the "Red Menace" from communist North Korea.

CONFLICT IN KOREA

In June 1950, communist North Korea invaded South Korea. The USSR backed North Korea. To prevent the spread of communism, the United States, with support from the United Nations, aided South Korea. The media, especially television, showed frightening scenes from Korean cities and jungles. Each side claimed it was fighting for the people there.

29

THE COLD WAR DEEPENS

The Cold War spread into many types of media, including books, movies, and television and radio programs. In a new style of mass communication, millions of leaflets were dropped from aircraft, telling the people who picked them up which side they should support. The Cold War would continue into the 1960s and bring the world to the brink of nuclear attack.

U. S. Senator Joseph McCarthy's anticommunist campaign was exposed, on television, as bitter and personal.

· TIME LINE ·

	WORLD EVENTS	HEADLINES	MEDIA EVENTS	TECHNOLOGY	THE ARTS
1940	•World War II continues (1939–1945)	•Churchill becomes British prime minister	•Churchill's radio speeches lift war-torn British spirits	•Regular FM radio broadcasts begin	•Walt Disney: Fantasia •First Bugs Bunny cartoon
1941	•Nazis invade Russia	•Japanese attack Pearl Harbor; U.S. enters war	•U.S.: radio broadcasts Pearl Harbor attack	•Hans Haas pioneers underwater photography	•Orson Welles stars in Citizen Kane
1942	•India: Gandhi imprisoned	•Japan suffers first major defeat at Midway	•U.S.: war censorship bans ad-lib street interviews	•Kodak makes first true color negative film	•Bergman and Bogart star in Casablanca
1943	•German forces surrender at Stalingrad	•Mussolini arrested •Zoot suit riots in U.S.	•U.S.: ABC network founded	•SCUBA gear improves underwater filming	•Jean-Paul Sartre: Being and Nothingness
1944	•Poland: Warsaw uprising crushed	•Allies land in France and drive back Germans	•U.S.: bandleader Glenn Miller, and plane, vanish	•IBM Mark 1 (first digital computer)	•Graham and Copland: Appalachian Spring (ballet)
1945	•Germany and Japan surrender; WWII ends	•Atomic bombs destroy Hiroshima and Nagasaki	•Americans sit by radios to attend FDR's funeral	•Arthur Clarke suggests communication satellites	•Steinbeck: Cannery Row •Britten: Peter Grimes
1946	•UN General Assembly holds first meetings	•Atomic bomb tested at Bikini Atoll	•Lord Haw-Haw executed for treason	•ENIAC (first modern electronic computer)	•France: first Cannes Film Festival
1947	•India and Pakistan gain independence	•McCarthy investigations affect movie industry	•Magnum Photos founded	•Bell Laboratories invents transistors	•The Diary of Anne Frank
1948	•S. Africa: apartheid •State of Israel founded	•Gandhi assassinated	•CBS and NBC begin nightly TV newscasts	•CBS develops 33-rpm long play records (LPs)	•John Huston: Key Largo
1949	•Germany forms East and West states	•USSR tests its first atomic bomb	•U.S.: Network TV begins	•RCA develops 45-rpm singles	•Arthur Miller: Death of a Salesman
1950	•Korean War begins •China invades Tibet	•U.S. begins development of hydrogen bomb	•I Love Lucy TV show begins	•Phonevision (early pay-per-view television)	•Disney uses real actors in Treasure Island
1951	•Libya becomes an independent country	•UN proposes cease-fire in Korea	•U.S.: first coast-to-coast TV broadcasts	•U.S.: first color television broadcast	•CBS begins See It Now with Edward Murrow
1952	•Kenya: Mau Mau revolt begins	•U.S.: Eisenhower elected president	•U.S. Supreme Court gives movies freedom of speech	•Sony sells first transistor radios	•Gary Cooper stars in High Noon
1953	•Korean War ends •USSR: Stalin dies	•Elizabeth II crowned Queen of England	•TV Guide prints first issue (1.5 million copies)	•U.S. tests Conelrad emergency radio system	•Arthur Miller: The Crucible
1954	•West Germany admitted to NATO	•U.S.: McCarthy's witch-hunt exposed on TV	•Sports Illustrated magazine founded	•Swanson introduces frozen TV dinners	•Akira Kurosawa: The Seven Samurai
1955	•South Africa leaves UN •Warsaw Pact formed	•Salk announces successful antipolio vaccine	•NBC-TV's Peter Pan has record number of viewers	•Tests begin on fiber optics digital communication	•James Dean stars in East of Eden
1956	•Suez Canal crisis in the Middle East	•South Vietnam becomes an independent republic	•CBS news videotaped for delayed broadcast	•Bell Labs tests PicturePhone	•Elvis Presley: "Heartbreak Hotel"
1957	•European Common Market (EEC) founded	•Soviet Union launches Sputnik I satellite	•U.S.: TV quiz-show fraud exposed	•FORTRAN (first high-level computer language	•Kerouac: On the Road •Bernstein: West Side Story
1958	•Iraq: coup forms independent republic	•"Ban the Bomb" anti-nuclear campaigns begin	•U.S.: United Press International formed	•Explorer I is first successful U.S. satellite	•Harold Pinter: The Birthday Party
1959	•Castro comes to power in Cuba	•Soviet premier Krushchev visits U.S.	•Mattel's Barbie dolls set sales record	•First silicon microchips start computer revolution	•Marilyn Monroe stars in Some Like It Hot

30

GLOSSARY

anchorman: the main person who reads news reports and introduces reports presented by others on a radio or television broadcast.

broadcast: send out, or transmit, to many people at the same time in the form of electromagnetic waves, or radio waves.

correspondent: a person employed by a newspaper, magazine, news agency, or broadcasting network to report news, usually from a distant location.

McCarthy era: a period in U. S. history, from 1950 to about 1954, during which U. S. Senator Joseph R. McCarthy had government officials, business leaders, and the media publicly investigated for un-American activities and communist sympathies.

periodicals: newspapers, magazines, and other print materials published consecutively with a fixed time period, such as daily or monthly, between issues.

phosphor: a substance that gives off, or emits, light in reacting to energy radiated in the form of waves or particles such as electrons.

photojournalism: the technique of presenting news using mostly photographs with captions, rather than full text with only a few photographs.

studio: a large room equipped for producing and broadcasting radio and television programs. Also, the general name for a large motion picture company.

transistor: a small electronic device, about the size of an eraser on a pencil, that contains at least three electrodes and controls the flow of electricity in radios, televisions, and other electronic equipment.

valve: a vacuum tube, consisting of a bulb-shaped glass container with two or more metal plates called electrodes inside, used to control electronic signals in early radios and TV sets.

MORE BOOKS TO READ

The 1950s: Music. The Century Kids (series). Dorothy and Tom Hoobler (Millbrook Press)

Cameras on the Battlefield: Photos of War. Matt White (Capstone Press)

Film and TV. Modern Media (series). Chris Oxlade (Barrons)

A Golden Age: The Golden Age of Radio. Smithsonian Institution Odyssey (series). Martha Wickham (Soundprints)

The History of Rock and Roll. Adam Woog (Lucent Books)

Hollywood at War: The Motion Picture Industry and World War II. Charnan Simon (Franklin Watts)

Joseph McCarthy: The Misuse of Political Power. Daniel Cohen (Millbrook Press)

The Soldiers' Voice: The Story of Ernie Pyle. Trailblazers Biographies (series). Barbara O'Connor (Carolrhoda Books)

Through the Decades: The 1950s. A Cultural History of the United States (series). Stuart A. Kallen, editor (Lucent Books)

Walt Disney's Fantasia. John Culhane (Harry Abrams)

WEB SITES

Fifties Web. *www.fiftiesweb.com/fifties.htm*

The Great Debate. *www.mbcnet.org/debateweb/html/greatdebate*

Sarah's Transistor Radios. *www.transistor.org*

TV Guide@50. *www.tvguide.com/50th*

The Walt Disney Studios: Studio History. *disney.go.com/StudioOperations/Welcome/history.html*

Due to the dynamic nature of the Internet, some web sites stay current longer than others. To find additional web sites, use a reliable search engine with one or more of the following keywords: *disk jockeys, Lord Haw-Haw, Marshall McLuhan, musicals, Elvis Presley, Ernie Pyle, quiz shows, television history, transistors,* and *World War II media.*

INDEX